Collins
MUSIC

T0312392

Singing
FRENCH

22 PHOTOCOPIABLE SONGS AND CHANTS FOR LEARNING FRENCH

HELEN MACGREGOR &
STEPHEN CHADWICK

Contents

Published by Collins
An imprint of HarperCollins*Publishers* Ltd
The News Building
1 London Bridge Street
London
SE1 9GF

HarperCollins*Publishers*
1st Floor Watermarque Building
Ringsend Road
Dublin 4
Ireland

www.collins.co.uk

Copyright © Helen MacGregor and Stephen Chadwick 2004
CD © HarperCollins*Publishers* Ltd 2004

ISBN-13: 978-0-7136-6898-8
Edited by Lucy Poddington and Emily Wilson
Designed by Jocelyn Lucas
Cover illustration © Emma Harding 2004
Inside illustrations © Joy Gosney 2004
CD produced by Stephen Chadwick at 3D Music Ltd
Performed by Marie Martin and Mehdi Benjelloun
Music set by Jeanne Fisher

Printed in Great Britain by Caligraving Ltd, Thetford, Norfolk.

A CIP catalogue record for this book is available from the British Library.

10 9 8 7 6

MIX
Paper from
responsible sources
FSC™ C007454

This book is produced from independently certified FSC™ paper
to ensure responsible forest management.

For more information visit: **www.harpercollins.co.uk/green**

Introduction

Singing French supports the teaching of French to beginners through an exciting new collection of songs and chants. It is intended for French teachers and parents with French language skills of any level.

The CD comprises performance tracks sung by native French speakers and backing tracks for every song, as well as teaching tracks for many of the songs giving spoken pronunciation reference for key vocabulary. The book contains photocopiable song words for each song and chant and teaching ideas which develop children's abilities to communicate in French and to appreciate French culture. No music reading is required to use the resource. However, melody lines are provided at the back of the book for music readers.

The resource links closely with the Qualifications and Curriculum Authority (QCA) guidelines and scheme of work for teaching Modern Foreign Languages (MFL) in primary, middle and special schools at Key Stage Two. It can also be used to support French teaching at Key Stage Three for pupils who have had little or no prior teaching of the language.

The songs, chants and activity ideas in **Singing French** help children to:

- enjoy and become familiar with the sounds of the French language;

- develop language skills and language-learning skills;

- become confident in speaking, understanding and reading a new language;

- learn about French culture and people.

Using the songs and chants

Each song or chant links to one or more aspects of language content from the QCA MFL scheme of work. The songs can be taught in any order to complement your teaching, but are arranged progressively in the book, with the later songs building on vocabulary already learnt and containing less repetition of words and phrases.

To familiarise children with the sounds of the French language and to develop good listening and aural memory skills, it is generally advisable to teach the songs using the CD or by singing them yourself before introducing the children to the written words. It is important to revisit the songs with sufficient frequency over a period of time for the children to become confident with the language.

The CD track numbers are referred to at appropriate points throughout the teaching notes and a full track list can be found on page 64. Towards the end of the CD, you will find teaching tracks giving pronunciation guidance for key words and phrases from the later songs. These can be used when teaching the song vocabulary. The CD is designed to work in all modern CD players; however, if your CD player does not play the last few teaching tracks, you will be able to play them through a computer.

Guidance is given for each of the songs and chants about possible ways of teaching and performing them, for example:

- by joining in with the chorus on first listening, then gradually learning the verses;

- by performing in two groups;

- by inviting smaller groups or soloists to perform parts.

The resource is designed to be used flexibly so that you can adapt the songs and activities to cater for the age, ability and experience of the children.

Once the songs have been learnt, they can be sung regularly at any time, either with the backing track or unaccompanied. Many songs lend themselves to adding actions, dance steps and/or percussion accompaniments, and could be incorporated into music lessons. If the children develop songs by writing their own verses, performances could be recorded for discussion and evaluation.

Developing the vocabulary

For each song or chant, ideas are provided of ways to extend learning using the song vocabulary as a starting point. These activities may be completed at the same time as learning the song or may be used at a later stage. Often the children are asked to compose their own verses to perform with the backing track, offering opportunities for differentiation and independent learning.

Key vocabulary for each song is given in the vocabulary box, with translations. The children could be encouraged to research further vocabulary using dictionaries.

Follow-up work

Linked to each song or chant are suggestions for games, role plays, research projects and cross-curricular activities to further the children's knowledge of French language and culture. These activities often involve combining vocabulary from a range of topics.

Many of the follow-up ideas can be used as extension activities for the more confident pupils, either working individually or in small groups. Other suggestions are suitable for use with the whole class, perhaps at a later stage, to consolidate and extend their learning. The activities incorporate reading, writing and use of ICT, and make other cross-curricular links with subjects such as Geography, PSHE and Citizenship.

Photocopiable song words

When the children are able to sing a song confidently (or at a later stage), you can introduce them to the written song words on the photocopiable sheets. These can be used in a variety of ways to support the development of literacy in the language. For example, the sheet could be:

- displayed as a song sheet on an OHT or interactive whiteboard;

- enlarged and displayed on the classroom wall as a poster;

- used in a lesson focusing on reading and writing;

- presented as a stimulus for composing new verses.

Resources

Very few additional resources are required in order to learn the songs and use the teaching ideas. Many of the illustrations on the photocopiable song sheets can be enlarged to make lively visual aids. Photocopiable number cards for use when learning numbers can be found on pages 62–63. Please note that any material not marked 'photocopiable' may not be photocopied.

When using the suggestions for developing the vocabulary and follow-up work, try to ensure that the children have access to French–English dictionaries so that they can look up additional vocabulary.

Once the songs have been learnt, they can be easily performed unaccompanied if a CD player is not available.

Melody lines

Melody lines are provided at the back of the book for music readers. Teachers or pupils may wish to play the melody lines on a piano when composing new verses.

Pronunciation

Occasionally word endings in the songs are given extra emphasis to fit in with the rhythm. Examples include:

Je vais en France pendant les vacances (Les vacances);
Où est le stade s'il vous plaît (Où est-il?).

In these cases, the teaching tracks at the end of the CD give the natural spoken pronunciation.

Bonjour

saying hello and goodbye/asking how someone is

CD tracks **1** the song **2** backing track

Using the song

All listen to the song (track 1). Ask the children to identify any words they recognise, such as **Bonjour**.

Teach the vocabulary either by listening to the song or by saying the words yourself for the children to copy. Ensure that everyone knows the meaning of the words in each line.

Learn to sing one line of the song at a time. (Listen to the rap sections without joining in.) When the class is familiar with the whole song, sing it with the backing track (track 2).

Developing the vocabulary

With your class, listen to the spoken greetings and farewells in the rap sections (track 1). Ask the children to count how many times each word or phrase is repeated. Together, identify the sequence in which they appear.

To introduce the class to the written words, write each of the phrases on the board or display an enlarged copy of the photocopiable song sheet. Invite an individual to come out and point to each phrase as it is spoken during the rap section.

Introduce other vocabulary that may be used in greetings or farewells,
eg **Bonjour Madame/Monsieur!** (used when greeting an adult)
Bienvenue! (Welcome!)
Ça va très bien, merci. Et tu? (I'm very well, thank you. And you?)

Comment ça va?

vocabulary

Bonjour! – Hello/Good morning/Good afternoon!

Ça va?/Comment ça va? – How are you?

Salut! – Hi!

Au revoir! – Goodbye!

Bonsoir! – Good evening/Goodnight!

Follow-up work

In small groups, the children choose greetings or farewells to devise a new rap for the song. Each group rehearses its new rap with the backing track (track 2). Encourage the groups to act out a scene while practising the rap.

The groups take it in turns to perform their rap to the class with the backing track. All join in singing the song each time.

Each group then records its new rap by drawing a cartoon strip of the scene with the vocabulary in speech bubbles.

Once the children are familiar with the next song, **Comment t'appelles-tu?**, they can add extra pictures and speech bubbles to their cartoon strips using this vocabulary.

Bonjour

Bonjour! Bonjour! Bonjour! Ça va? Comment ça va? Salut! Salut! Salut! Au revoir! Bonsoir! Bonsoir!

(rap) Bonjour! Bonjour! Ça va? Ça va? Comment ça va?

Bonjour! Bonjour! Ça va? Ça va? Ça va? Comment ça va?

Bonjour! Bonjour! Ça va? Ça va? Comment ça va?

Bonjour! Bonjour! Ça va? Ça va? Ça va? Comment ça va?

Bonjour! Bonjour! Bonjour! Ça va? Comment ça va? Salut! Salut! Salut! Au revoir! Bonsoir! Bonsoir!

(rap) Salut! Salut! Salut! Salut! Salut! Salut!

Au revoir! Au revoir! Bonsoir! Bonsoir!

Salut! Salut! Salut! Salut! Salut! Salut!

Au revoir! Au revoir! Bonsoir! Bonsoir!

Bonjour! Bonjour! Bonjour! Ça va? Comment ça va? Salut! Salut! Salut! Au revoir! Bonsoir! Bonsoir!

Comment t'appelles-tu?

introducing oneself/asking how someone is

CD tracks **3** the song **4** backing track

Using the song

Listen to the song (track 3) with the class, then teach the phrases either using the song or by saying the words yourself for the children to copy. Ensure that everyone is confident with the responses to the questions, eg

Comment t'appelles-tu? Je m'appelle Charlotte. Comment ça va? Ça va très bien, merci.

Ask the children if they can tell you the three names heard in the song (Mehdi, Marie and Lucas).

Using the backing track (track 4), sing the part of the leader (shown in bold on the photocopiable song sheet). Choose a child to shake hands with as you sing **Comment t'appelles-tu?** The chosen child sings the response, inserting his or her name. Sing the next line yourself using the child's name and continue with **Comment ça va**, answered by the soloist. Repeat the song several times, choosing different members of the class in turn.

When everyone is confident singing the song, divide into two groups and stand in two facing circles, one inside the other. Each pair of facing children shakes hands as the outer circle leads the song and the inner circle sings the responses. At the end of each verse, the inner circle moves clockwise one place so that everyone meets a new partner. Performing the song without the backing track allows as many repeats as you wish.

Swap parts so that the children in the inner circle have a chance to lead the song.

Developing the vocabulary

As a class, practise alternative ways of greeting people and responding, eg

Comment tu t'appelles? (What is your name?)
Salut! (Hi!)　　　**Ça va?** (How are you?)
Oui, ça va. (I'm fine.)　　**Pas mal!** (Not bad!)

Make a collection of French name cards, eg **Caroline**, **Nathalie**, **Emilie**, **David**, **Jamel**, **Marc** and so on. Practise the pronunciation of the names with the class. Divide the class into small groups, allocating a name card to each child. Each group acts out a scene using greeting and farewell vocabulary. Invite the groups to present their scenes to the class.

vocabulary

Comment t'appelles-tu? – What is your name?

Je m'appelle ... – My name is ...

Bonjour! – Hello/Good morning/Good afternoon!

Comment ça va? – How are you?

Ça va très bien, merci. – I am very well, thank you.

Follow-up work

Teach the vocabulary for naming other people or groups of people:
Il s'appelle ...
Elle s'appelle ...
Ils s'appellent ...
Elles s'appellent ...

When the children have learnt the vocabulary for members of the family, they can ask questions to find out the names of each other's parents, brothers and sisters, eg
Comment s'appelle ton père/ta sœur?
(What is your dad/sister called?)

Tell the children that they can ask what an object is called by saying **Comment s'appelle-t-il?**

Comment t'appelles-tu?

Comment t'appelles-tu?

Comment t'appelles-tu?

☺ Je m'appelle ....

Bonjour, ... !

Comment ça va?

Comment ça va?

☺ Ça va très bien, merci.

Comment t'appelles-tu?

Comment t'appelles-tu?

☺ Je m'appelle ....

Bonjour, ... !

Comment ça va?

Comment ça va?

☺ Ça va très bien, merci.

Comment t'appelles-tu?

Comment t'appelles-tu?

☺ Je m'appelle ....

Bonjour, ... !

Comment ça va?

Comment ça va?

☺ Ça va très bien, merci.

Ça va très bien, merci.

SINGING FRENCH © HELEN MACGREGOR & STEPHEN CHADWICK 2004, HarperCollins*Publishers* Ltd

Un deux trois

CD tracks **5** the song **6** backing track

Using the song

Listen to the song several times (track 5), then all join in singing the words **un deux trois** in each verse. As you sing each number, hold up the correct number of fingers.

Teach the rest of the vocabulary to the class either using the song or by saying the words yourself for the children to copy. You might like to show the class the pictures on the photocopiable song sheet as you practise the vocabulary, to reinforce the meaning of the words.

Practise singing the song with track 5, without using the song sheet. When the class is familiar with the whole song, sing it with the backing track (track 6).

Developing the vocabulary

As a class, make up new verses using other animal names, eg

J'ai trois souris (mice)

J'ai trois hamsters (hamsters)

J'ai trois chevaux (horses)

J'ai trois vaches (cows)

All sing the new verses with the backing track (track 6).

If you wish, discuss regular and irregular plurals with the class. For regular plurals, simply add an 's'. Words already ending in 's' do not change, eg **un souris/trois souris**. Some nouns form irregular plurals, eg **un cheval/trois chevaux**.

Once the children have developed a wider range of vocabulary, encourage them to compose new verses with other themes, eg

J'ai trois sœurs/frères (Family)

J'ai trois gommes/stylos (School)

J'ai trois glaces/gâteaux (Food)

vocabulary

un – one

deux – two

trois – three

Oh là là! – exclamation, eg Oh my goodness!

Regardez-moi! – Look at me!

j'ai – I have

trois chiens (un chien) – three dogs (a dog)

trois chats (un chat) – three cats (a cat)

trois poissons (un poisson) – three fish (a fish)

trois lapins (un lapin) – three rabbits (a rabbit)

Follow-up work

Adapt the song words to practise conjugating the verb avoir:

j'ai
tu as
il/elle a
nous avons
vous avez
ils/elles ont

For example:

Oh là là!
Regarde là-bas! (Look over there!)
Elle a trois chiens (She has three dogs) Un deux trois.

Oh là là!
Regarde là-bas!
Ils ont trois chats (They have three cats) Un deux trois.

Un deux trois

Oh là là!
Regardez-moi!
J'ai trois chiens
Un deux trois.

Oh là là!
Regardez-moi!
J'ai trois chats
Un deux trois.

Oh là là!
Regardez-moi!
J'ai trois poissons
Un deux trois.

Oh là là!
Regardez-moi!
J'ai trois lapins
Un deux trois.

Un deux trois!

SINGING FRENCH © HELEN MACGREGOR & STEPHEN CHADWICK 2004, HarperCollins*Publishers* Ltd

11

A douze

CD tracks  the song  backing track

Using the song

Photocopy the number cards on pages 62–63 and use them to make a number track from one to twelve. (For numbers 11 and 12, make multiple copies of the number 10 and layer the appropriate digit over the zero.)

Explain to the children that they are going to learn the numbers from one to twelve. Listen to the song (track 7), pointing to each number on the number track as it occurs in the song.

Sing the song several times until everyone is confident with the vocabulary, alternating between track 7 and the backing track (track 8) as necessary.

All learn the body percussion accompaniment shown on the photocopiable song sheet: clap click click. Perform it in time with track 7. Then divide the class into two groups: group one sings the song with the backing track while group two performs the accompaniment. Swap parts to let group one perform the accompaniment.

With practice, everyone should be able to perform the accompaniment at the same time as singing the song.

Developing the vocabulary

When the class is confident with the song, all try singing it backwards:

**Dix neuf huit
sept six cinq
quatre trois deux
un.**

**Douze onze dix
neuf huit sept
six cinq quatre
trois deux un.**

Introduce the class to the question **Quel âge as-tu?** (How old are you?) and the response, eg **J'ai dix ans** (I am ten).

vocabulary

à douze – up to twelve
un – one
deux – two
trois – three
quatre – four
cinq – five
six – six
sept – seven
huit – eight
neuf – nine
dix – ten
onze – eleven
douze – twelve
répétez – repeat

Follow-up work

Make a set of number cards from one to twelve using the photocopiable number cards on pages 62–63. Select twelve children to stand in a line facing the class and allocate a number card to each child, which they hold up for the class to see.

Invite an individual to put the children into a different order to make a new number sequence, eg

1 3 5 7 9 11 2 4 6 8 10 12

As the individual points to each card in turn, the class chants the new number sequence. When everyone is confident, sing it with the backing track (track 8). Repeat the activity to give others a turn at composing number sequences.

To familiarise the class with the written number words, repeat the activity using cards which show the numbers in words instead of figures. (Alternatively, write the number words on the board.)

A douze

Un   deux   trois
quatre   cinq   six
sept   huit   neuf
dix.

Un   deux   trois
quatre   cinq   six
sept   huit   neuf
dix.

Un   deux   trois
quatre   cinq   six
sept   huit   neuf
dix   onze   douze.

Un   deux   trois
quatre   cinq   six
sept   huit   neuf
dix.

....
répétez
....

Un   deux   trois
quatre   cinq   six
sept   huit   neuf
dix.

photocopiable

Ma trousse

Using the song

Listen to the song (track 9) and teach it verse by verse, holding up actual classroom objects to illustrate the vocabulary. Practise the names of the objects using track 45 or by saying the words yourself for the children to copy.

Draw attention to the masculine and feminine nouns, eg

un crayon/le crayon

une gomme/la gomme

As the list at the end of each verse grows, remind the class of the order by selecting individuals to come to the front and hold up the ruler, eraser, pencil sharpener, pencil or pen as each word is sung.

vocabulary

ma trousse – my pencil case
dans – in
j'ai – I have
un stylo – a pen
pour écrire – to write with
un crayon – a pencil
et – and
un taille-crayon – a pencil sharpener
une gomme – an eraser
une règle – a ruler

Developing the vocabulary

As a class, extend the song by adding items from the children's own pencil cases, eg

une feutre (a felt-tip)   **de la colle** (some glue)

une calculatrice (a calculator)   **des ciseaux** (scissors)

When the class is familiar with the vocabulary, practise asking individuals the following question:

Dans ta trousse, qu'est-ce que tu as?
Montres-moi, s'il te plaît.

The individual holds up an item and gives their response, eg

Dans ma trousse, j'ai une gomme.

The children may repeat this activity in pairs, taking it in turns to ask each other the question.

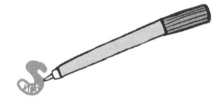

Follow-up work

Select a classroom object and show it to the class, asking **Qu'est-ce que c'est?** (What is it?). The class or an individual responds by identifying the object, eg **C'est un crayon.**

When the children have been introduced to the vocabulary for colours, they may add the appropriate colour, eg **C'est un crayon noir.** Remind the children that the colour adjective always comes after the noun.

Discuss that an 'e' is added to the adjectives **bleu, noir, vert** and **gris** when the noun is feminine. This may affect the way the word is pronounced, eg **un crayon vert** (m), **une feutre verte** (f). Note that **blanc/ blanche** is irregular, eg **un crayon blanc** (m), **une gomme blanche** (f).

Ma trousse

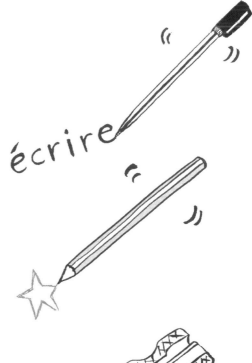

Dans ma trousse, j'ai un stylo.

Dans ma trousse, j'ai un stylo.

Un stylo pour écrire.

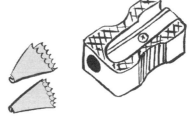

Dans ma trousse, j'ai un crayon.

Dans ma trousse, j'ai un crayon.

Un crayon

Et un stylo pour écrire.

Dans ma trousse, j'ai un taille-crayon.

Dans ma trousse, j'ai un taille-crayon.

Un taille-crayon, un crayon

Et un stylo pour écrire.

Dans ma trousse, j'ai une gomme.

Dans ma trousse, j'ai une gomme.

Une gomme, un taille-crayon, un crayon

Et un stylo pour écrire.

Dans ma trousse, j'ai une règle.

Dans ma trousse, j'ai une règle.

Une règle, une gomme, un taille-crayon, un crayon

Et un stylo pour écrire.

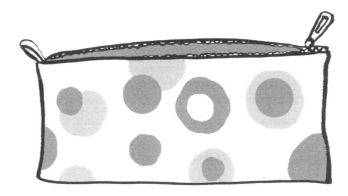

SINGING FRENCH © HELEN MACGREGOR & STEPHEN CHADWICK 2004, HarperCollins*Publishers* Ltd

La semaine

CD tracks  the song  backing track

Using the song

Explain to the children that they are going to learn the names of the days of the week. All listen to the song (track 11), joining in with the counting phrases in the chorus when they are repeated (**Un deux trois ... Les sept jours de la semaine**).

Teach the vocabulary for the days of the week, either by listening to the song or by saying the words yourself for the children to copy.

Sing the whole song several times until everyone is confident with the vocabulary.

Developing the vocabulary

Make an enlarged photocopy of the days of the week cards on the song sheet. Display the cards and point to each in turn as you all sing the song. Explain that lower case letters are used in French for the days of the week (except when starting sentences and lines of a song etc).

Using the backing track (track 12), start on a different day of the week and sing through the sequence in order, eg **mardi, mercredi, jeudi ...**, pointing to the appropriate cards. Repeat the activity, starting on other days.

Introduce the class to the following vocabulary:

C'est quel jour, aujourd'hui? (What day is it today?) **Aujourd'hui, c'est ...** (Today it's ...)

Et hier/demain? (And yesterday/tomorrow?)

le week-end (the weekend)

vocabulary

la semaine – the week
lundi – Monday
mardi – Tuesday
mercredi – Wednesday
jeudi – Thursday
vendredi – Friday
samedi – Saturday
dimanche – Sunday
un – one
deux – two
trois – three
quatre – four
cinq – five
six – six
sept – seven
les jours (un jour) – the days (a day)
de la semaine – of the week

Follow-up work

Photocopy and cut out sets of the days of the week cards on the song sheet. Then cut each card in two, splitting the words as follows: **lu-ndi, ma-rdi, mer-credi, jeu-di, ven-dredi, sa-medi, di-manche**.

Give pairs of children a set of the cards each for them to match up the parts of the words correctly. All listen to track 11 for the pairs to check their answers.

Invite the children to design a personal diary (**un journal**) for one week, writing the days of the week in French and drawing real or imaginary events for each day. Remind them to use lower case letters, eg **lundi**.

La semaine

Lundi

Mardi

Mercredi

Jeudi

Vendredi

Samedi

Dimanche

Un deux trois quatre cinq six sept,

Les sept jours de la semaine.

Un deux trois quatre cinq six sept,

Les sept jours de la semaine.

Lundi …

Un deux trois quatre cinq six sept …

Lundi …

SINGING FRENCH © HELEN MACGREGOR & STEPHEN CHADWICK 2004, HarperCollins*Publishers* Ltd

Onze à vingt

CD tracks   **13** the song   **14** backing track

Using the song

Make a set of number cards from eleven to twenty using the photocopiable number cards on pages 62–63. (To do this, make multiple copies of number 10 and layer other digits over the tens or units digit as appropriate.) Display the cards as a number track. Listen to the song (track 13) with the class, pointing to each number on the number track as it occurs in the song.

Teach the vocabulary either by listening to the song or by saying the numbers yourself for the children to copy. Then all join in echo-singing the song: listen to the numbers sung by the female singer and join in with the echo (male singer).

When everyone is confident singing the song, divide into two groups to echo-sing the song with the backing track (track 14). Swap parts so that each group has an opportunity to lead the song.

vocabulary

onze à vingt – from eleven to twenty
onze – eleven
douze – twelve
treize – thirteen
quatorze – fourteen
quinze – fifteen
seize – sixteen
dix-sept – seventeen
dix-huit – eighteen
dix-neuf – nineteen
vingt – twenty

Developing the vocabulary

All sit in a circle. Take turns to chant a number, starting at eleven and finishing at twenty. Repeat several times around the circle, then include all the numbers from one to twenty.

Make a set of number cards from one to twenty. Shuffle the cards, then hold one up for the class to see, asking **C'est combien?** (How many is this?). The class or an individual responds, eg **Treize**.

Play **Loto** (Bingo) with the class. Each child draws a grid of twelve squares and writes in any twelve numbers between one and twenty. Shuffle a set of number cards from one to twenty, then call out numbers in French one at a time. When the children hear a number they have written down, they cross it off their grid. The first child to cross off all twelve numbers shouts **Loto** and wins the game. The winner may become the next caller when you play the game again.

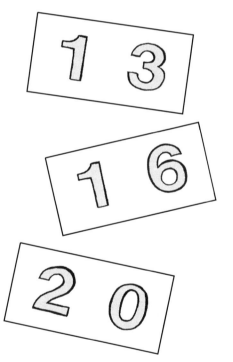

Follow-up work

Play mental maths games using number cards from one to twenty. Select two cards and hold them up for the class to see. Ask addition questions, eg

J'ai dix et j'ai deux. C'est combien?

(I have ten and two. How many is that?)

Make additions with answers above twenty and ask if anyone can work out how to say the answer, eg **vingt-trois** (twenty-three).

Teach the class additional vocabulary, eg

vingt et un (twenty-one)   **trente** (thirty)

trente et un (thirty-one)

Play the game again using a combination of cards showing numbers in figures and words, eg **19** and **deux**. (Alternatively, write the numbers on the board.) To answer the question, individuals may say the answer or select the matching number word card.

Onze à vingt

Onze douze treize, quatorze quinze seize.

Onze douze treize, quatorze quinze seize.

Dix-sept	Dix-sept
Dix-huit	Dix-huit
Dix-neuf	Dix-neuf
Vingt!	Vingt!

Onze douze treize, quatorze quinze seize.

Onze douze treize, quatorze quinze seize.

Dix-sept	Dix-sept
Dix-huit	Dix-huit
Dix-neuf	Dix-neuf
Vingt!	Vingt!

Onze douze treize, quatorze quinze seize.

Onze douze treize, quatorze quinze seize.

Dix-sept	Dix-sept
Dix-huit	Dix-huit
Dix-neuf	Dix-neuf
Vingt!	Vingt!

L'alphabet

CD tracks  **15** the chant   **16** backing track

Using the chant

Show the class an enlarged copy of the alphabet on the photocopiable song sheet.

Listen to the chant (track 15), pointing to each letter in turn to familiarise the class with the letter names. All practise the pronunciation, either using the chant or by saying the letter names yourself for the children to copy. Ensure that everyone understands the meaning of the vocabulary in the rap sections.

Repeat the chant until everyone is confident. Then invite a child to conduct by pointing to the letters in turn as the class performs to the backing track (track 16).

vocabulary

l'alphabet – the alphabet
c'est – it is
français – French

Developing the vocabulary

Play **Le pendu** (Hangman) with the class. Select a French word from vocabulary already learnt, such as a day of the week. Mark on the board the number of letters it contains, eg _ _ _ _ _ _ _ _ (**vendredi**).

Going round the class in turn, invite individuals to suggest a letter name in French. Continue the game as you would play Hangman in English. The first child to identify the word correctly may choose the next word to lead the game.

Follow-up work

Revise the following vocabulary:

Comment tu t'appelles?/Comment t'appelles-tu?

Je m'appelle ...

Teach the question **Comment ça s'écrit?** (How do you spell that?). Give the children the opportunity to practise spelling their names in French. Some may be able to spell both first name and surname.

Make several French name cards, eg **Marie, Sabine, Jeanne, Pierre, Tarik, Lucas**. (Use common names with no accents.) Give the cards to individuals, who take turns to spell out their French name as the class writes down the letters. All practise the pronunciations of the names and compare the written answers with the cards to check spellings.

L'alphabet

(rap) L'alphabet! C'est l'alphabet français!

L'alphabet! C'est l'alphabet français!

A B C D E F G
H I J K L M N O P
Q R S T U V W
X Y Z

(rap) L'alphabet! C'est l'alphabet français!

L'alphabet! C'est l'alphabet français!

L'alphabet! C'est l'alphabet français!

A B C D E F G...

(rap) L'alphabet! C'est l'alphabet français!

L'alphabet! C'est l'alphabet français!

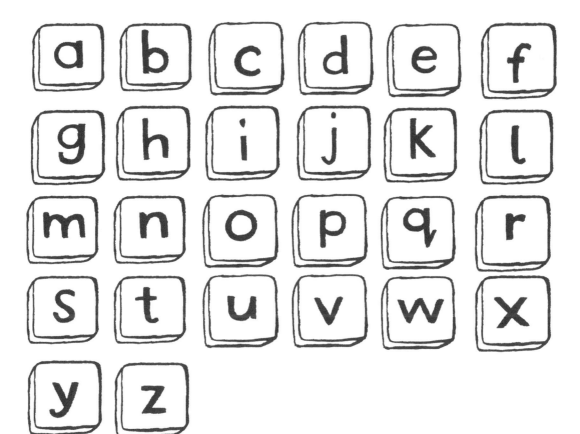

photocopiable

Ma famille

CD tracks  **17** the song  **18** backing track

Using the song

Enlarge and display the individual pictures of family members on the photocopiable song sheet. All listen to the song (track 17). Point to the family members in turn as the words **père**, **mère**, **sœur**, **frère** are sung.

Teach the vocabulary either by listening to the song or by saying the words yourself for the children to copy. Join in with the first two lines and chorus.

Practise the introductions part of the song (**Je te présente mon père ...**), dividing into two groups to match the female and male voices. Swap over so that everyone has a chance to sing both parts. When the children are confident, sing the song with the backing track (track 18).

Developing the vocabulary

Once the class is familiar with the song, choose four individuals to play the roles of Monsieur and Madame Petit, Stéphanie and Lucien. Choose a leader to play the 'moi' character, who introduces each of the family members to individuals in the class. They should respond with an appropriate greeting, eg **Bonjour Lucien!**

Introduce other vocabulary for members of the family, eg

ma grand-mère (my grandmother)

mon grand-père (my grandfather)

ma tante (my aunt)

mon oncle (my uncle)

mes parents (my parents)

ma petite sœur (my little sister)

mon frère aîné (my elder/eldest brother)

Encourage groups of children to practise introducing family members in role play.

vocabulary

ma famille – my family

mon père – my dad

ma mère – my mum

ma sœur – my sister

mon frère – my brother

c'est ma famille – this is my family

c'est moi – this is me

c'est la famille Petit – this is the Petit family

je te présente – I introduce to you

Bonjour! – Hello/Good morning/Good afternoon!

Monsieur Petit – Mr Petit

Madame Petit – Mrs Petit

Salut! – Hi!

Follow-up work

Ask the children to bring in photos or to draw portraits of people in their family. Each child prepares a presentation for the class using vocabulary already learnt, eg

J'ai une sœur. Elle s'appelle Samira. Elle a cinq ans.

(I have one sister. She is called Samira. She is five.)

J'ai deux sœurs. Elles s'appellent Amy et Jodie.

Remind the children that an 's' is added to nouns with regular plurals, eg **deux sœurs, deux frères**.

Introduce further vocabulary, if needed, eg

ma belle-mère (my stepmother)

mon beau-père (my stepfather)

ma demi-sœur (my stepsister)

mon demi-frère (my stepbrother)

Ma famille

Père, mère, sœur, frère.
Père, mère, sœur, frère.

C'est ma famille, c'est moi!
C'est la famille Petit, c'est ma famille!
C'est ma famille, c'est moi!
C'est la famille Petit, c'est ma famille!

Je te présente mon père.
Bonjour Monsieur Petit!
Je te présente ma mère.
Bonjour Madame Petit!
Je te présente ma sœur, Stéphanie.
Salut Stéphanie!
Je te présente mon frère, Lucien.
Salut Lucien!

C'est ma famille, c'est moi ...

SINGING FRENCH © HELEN MACGREGOR & STEPHEN CHADWICK 2004, HarperCollins*Publishers* Ltd

Mon monstre

names of parts of the body

Using the song

Enlarge and display the illustration of the monster on the photocopiable song sheet. Identify and count, in French, each of the body parts. Listen to the song (track 19) and point to the appropriate parts of your body as the words are sung, asking the class to copy you.

Teach the vocabulary for the monster-building verse (**Mon monstre a une tête ...**) using track 46 or by saying the words yourself for the children to copy. Then join in with this section of the song. Gradually learn the whole song to sing with the backing track (track 20).

Developing the vocabulary

Ask individuals or small groups to design and illustrate their own monster. Teach any additional singular vocabulary they may need, eg **une oreille, un œil, un bras, un nez**. If you wish, remind the children that an 's' is added to nouns with regular plurals, eg **deux têtes, deux bouches**. Introduce further vocabulary, eg

le corps (the body)

les épaules/une épaule (shoulders)

les genoux/un genou (knees)

le dos (the back)

les cheveux (hair)

Using their illustrations as a guide, the children practise singing a new monster-building verse, eg

**Mon monstre a quatre têtes,
Deux bras et une oreille ...**

Using the backing track (track 20), perform the song with the whole class singing **J'ai un copain ...** and individuals or small groups contributing their own monster-building verses.

vocabulary

mon monstre – my monster
j'ai – I have
un copain/une copine – a friend (m/f)
un bon copain/une bonne copine – a good friend (m/f)
unique – unique
vrai – genuine, true
quand – when
je suis seul/e – I am alone (m/f)
je le fais moi-même – I make him myself
c'est la méthode scientifique – it's the scientific method
mon monstre a – my monster has
une tête – a head/one head
quatre – four
les bras (un bras) – arms (an arm)
et – and
six – six
les oreilles (une oreille) – ears
les mains (une main) – hands
deux – two
les jambes (une jambe) – legs
les pieds (un pied) – feet
une bouche – a mouth/one mouth
cinq – five
les dents (une dent) – teeth
huit – eight
les yeux (un œil) – eyes
trois – three
les nez (un nez) – noses

Follow-up work

Display a large poster of a potato 'body' on the classroom wall, or use an OHT or interactive whiteboard. Invite individuals to draw body parts on the body to make a potato creature.

Ask the class to describe the creature, eg

Il a une tête, trois jambes et six pieds.

When the children have been introduced to the vocabulary for colours and the agreement of nouns and adjectives, they can design a monster, in colour, and prepare a presentation for the class, eg

Mon monstre a le nez rouge, les oreilles jaunes et la bouche verte.

(My monster has a red nose, yellow ears and a green mouth.)

Mon monstre

J'ai un copain, un bon copain unique, vrai, unique!

J'ai un copain, un bon copain unique, vrai, unique!

Quand je suis seul, je le fais moi-même,

C'est la méthode scientifique, méthode scientifique.

Quand je suis seul, je le fais moi-même,

C'est la méthode scientifique, méthode scientifique.

Mon monstre a une tête,

Quatre bras et six oreilles.

Mon monstre a quatre mains,

Deux jambes et deux pieds.

Mon monstre a une bouche,

Cinq dents, huit yeux et trois nez.

J'ai un copain, un bon copain unique, vrai, unique ...

J'ai un copain, un bon copain unique, vrai, unique!

Zéro à cent

Using the song

Explain to the children that they are going to learn to count in tens up to one hundred. After this, they are going to learn how to say all the numbers up to one hundred. All listen to the song (track 21) and gradually join in with counting in tens.

When the children are confident with this, introduce the numbers in the middle section of the song, explaining the rule of using **et un**. Contrast this with numbers with units from two to nine, eg **vingt-deux, trentetrois**. Teach the vocabulary either using the song or by saying the words yourself for the children to copy.

Sing the song with the backing track (track 22). During the **C'est combien?** section, sing the question yourself as a solo and hold up cards showing the numbers from the song in figures (or point to numbers written on the board). The class calls out the answer each time. Then make the activity more difficult by changing the order in which you hold up the cards, eg **vingt, cent, trente, quarante.**

Developing the vocabulary

Using the backing track (track 22), substitute other numbers during the **C'est combien?** section by holding up number cards or by writing numbers on the board. Start with tens, then when the children are confident extend to any numbers between zero and one hundred.

Invite eight children to choose numbers to write or hold up as **C'est combien?** is sung. The class responds by calling out the number each time.

Ask the children to work out larger numbers using the vocabulary they have learnt, eg

cent un (101)	**deux cents** (200)
cent deux (102)	**deux cent un** (201)
cent trois (103)	**deux cent deux** (202)

vocabulary

zéro à cent – from zero to a hundred
zéro – zero
dix – ten
vingt – twenty
trente – thirty
quarante – forty
cinquante – fifty
soixante – sixty
soixante-dix – seventy
quatre-vingts – eighty
quatre-vingt-dix – ninety
cent – one hundred
C'est combien? – How many is this?
vingt et un – twenty-one
vingt-deux – twenty-two
trente et un – thirty-one
trente-trois – thirty-three
quarante et un – forty-one
quarante-quatre – forty-four
cinquante et un – fifty-one
cinquante-cinq – fifty-five
soixante et un – sixty-one
soixante-six – sixty-six
soixante et onze – seventy-one
soixante-dix-sept – seventy-seven
quatre-vingt-un – eighty-one
quatre-vingt-huit – eighty-eight
quatre-vingt-onze – ninety-one
quatre-vingt-dix-neuf – ninety-nine
quarante-cinq – forty-five
soixante-douze – seventy-two
quatre-vingt-treize – ninety-three

Follow-up work

All sitting in a circle, practise counting round in tens from zero to one hundred. Extend to counting in ones from zero to one hundred.

When everyone is confident, count around the circle in ones starting at one hundred. Gradually build up a knowledge of larger numbers, introducing **mille** (one thousand). You could also practise counting backwards.

When topics such as food and clothing have been introduced, act out scenes in the market or supermarket using price cards and props. Practise vocabulary relating to the prices of goods, eg

C'est combien? (How much is it?)

Cent vingt-trois euros. (123 euros.)

Zéro à cent

Zéro, dix, vingt, trente, quarante, cinquante, soixante,
Soixante-dix, quatre-vingts, quatre-vingt-dix, cent! Zéro, dix,
vingt, trente, quarante, cinquante, soixante, Soixante-dix,
quatre-vingts, quatre-vingt-dix, cent!

photocopiable

C'est combien?   ......(Trente!)..........   **30**

C'est combien?   ......(Vingt!)..........   **20**

C'est combien?   ......(Quarante!).......   **40**

C'est combien?   ......(Cent!)...............   **100**

21 Vingt et un	Vingt-deux **22**	
31 Trente et un	Trente-trois **33**	
41 Quarante et un	Quarante-quatre **44**	
51 Cinquante et un	Cinquante-cinq **55**	
60 Soixante		
61 Soixante et un	Soixante-six **66**	
71 Soixante et onze	Soixante-dix-sept **77**	
81 Quatre-vingt-un	Quatre-vingt-huit **88**	
91 Quatre-vingt-onze	Quatre-vingt-dix-neuf **99**	
100 Cent!		

C'est combien?   ......(Trente et un!)...............   **31**

C'est combien?   ......(Quarante-cinq!).............   **45**

C'est combien?   ......(Soixante-douze!)............   **72**

C'est combien?   ......(Quatre-vingt-treize!)........   **93**

Zéro, dix, vingt, trente, quarante, cinquante, soixante ...

Joyeux anniversaire

months of the year/questions about birthdays

Using the song

Listen to the song (track 23) and all learn the names of the months. Explain that during the middle section anyone with a birthday in the relevant month calls out **Oui** after the month is named. The rest of the class responds by singing **Joyeux anniversaire!**

Practise the vocabulary for the rest of the song using track 47 or by saying the words yourself for the children to copy. Gradually learn the whole song to sing with the backing track (track 24).

Developing the vocabulary

Ask the children to work out how to say the day and month of their birthday, eg **Mon anniversaire, c'est le treize octobre**. If any children have birthdays on the first of the month, they will need to be told to use **premier** instead of **un**, eg **le premier mai**. Practise this by asking individuals **Quelle est la date de ton anniversaire?**

Teach the phrase **Quelle est ta date de naissance?** (What is your date of birth?). Ask them to work out how to say the day, month and year, eg

Ma date de naissance, c'est le sept février, mille neuf cent quatre-vingt-seize.

(My date of birth is 7 February 1996.)

Teach the children additional useful vocabulary, eg

un mois (a month)

un an/une année (a year)

un calendrier (a calendar)

Bonne Année (Happy New Year)

Joyeux Noël (Merry Christmas)

vocabulary

Joyeux anniversaire! – Happy birthday!

un anniversaire – a birthday

Quelle est la date de ton anniversaire? – What date is your birthday?

au printemps – in spring

en été – in summer

en automne – in autumn

en hiver – in winter

janvier – January

oui – yes

février – February

mars – March

avril – April

mai – May

juin – June

juillet – July

août – August

septembre – September

octobre – October

novembre – November

décembre – December

Follow-up work

Divide the class into groups and give one group a blank French calendar. Each child takes a turn to ask another group member when his or her birthday is, eg

Daniel, quelle est la date de ton anniversaire?

Daniel answers with the date of his birthday in French and the questioner writes Daniel's name on the relevant date of the calendar.

When the birthdays of everyone in the group are recorded on the calendar, it is passed in turn around the other groups. The completed calendar of class birthdays can be displayed in the classroom and used throughout the year to reinforce the vocabulary.

Joyeux anniversaire

Quelle est la date de ton anniversaire?

Quelle est la date de ton anniversaire?

Au printemps, en été, en automne, en hiver? Quelle

est la date de ton anniversaire?

Janvier	(Oui!)	Joyeux anniversaire!
Février	(Oui!)	Joyeux anniversaire!
Mars	(Oui!)	Joyeux anniversaire!
Avril	(Oui!)	Joyeux anniversaire!
Mai	(Oui!)	Joyeux anniversaire!
Juin	(Oui!)	Joyeux anniversaire!
Juillet	(Oui!)	Joyeux anniversaire!
Août	(Oui!)	Joyeux anniversaire!
Septembre	(Oui!)	Joyeux anniversaire!
Octobre	(Oui!)	Joyeux anniversaire!
Novembre	(Oui!)	Joyeux anniversaire!
Décembre	(Oui!)	Joyeux anniversaire!

Quelle est la date de ton anniversaire ...

Joyeux anniversaire

Où habites-tu?

the verb habiter/names of French towns

CD tracks   **25** the song   **26** backing track   **48** spoken phrases

Using the song

Listen to the song (track 25) and all join in with the chorus each time it is sung. Then teach the verses one at a time, either by listening to track 48 or by saying the words yourself for the children to copy. Explain any new vocabulary and point out that the adjectives **cool** and **super** are informally used among friends.

When the class is familiar with the song, divide into two groups to sing the verses or the chorus with the backing track (track 26). Swap parts so that everyone has an opportunity to sing the verses. If you wish, you can allocate four small groups one verse each, while the rest of the class sings the chorus.

Developing the vocabulary

Look at a map of France and identify several key towns and cities. (You could enlarge and display the map on page 38.) Invite the children to choose a place to live in, then ask individuals **Où habites-tu?** Help them to adapt vocabulary they have previously learnt to say something about their choice, eg

C'est en France. (It's in France.)

C'est au nord de la France. (It's in the north of France.)

C'est la capitale de la France. (It's the capital of France.)

Introduce the names of other countries, eg

au pays de Galles (in Wales)

en Ecosse (in Scotland)

en Irlande du Nord (in Northern Ireland)

en Espagne (in Spain)

en Italie (in Italy)

Each child chooses a town or city in one of these countries to live in (researching using maps or the internet if necessary). Ask individuals where they live. When they respond with the name of the town or city, ask **C'est dans quel pays?** (In which country is it?).

vocabulary

Où habites-tu?/Où est-ce que tu habites? – Where do you live?

j'habite – I live

à Londres – in London

c'est en Angleterre – it's in England

j'habite un appartement – I live in a flat

c'est au bord de la rivière – it's by the river

dis-moi – tell me

Paris est en France – Paris is in France

j'aime – I like

monter à la Tour Eiffel – to go up the Eiffel Tower

c'est très cool – it's really cool (informal)

j'ai de la chance – I'm lucky

au bord de la mer – by the sea

pêcher – to fish/fishing

avec – with

mon oncle – my uncle

les poissons, ils sont supers – the fish are great (informal)

la région du vin – the wine region

le vin blanc, rosé ou rouge – white, rosé or red wine

comme tu veux – whatever you like

les vins sont bons – wine is good

Follow-up work

Collect maps and tourist information about French towns and cities from the internet or tourist information centres. Encourage small groups to investigate and list key attractions and features of different places, eg

Paris: la Seine, la Tour Eiffel, l'Arc de Triomphe, le Louvre

The groups then tell the class what they have found out, eg

A Paris on peut visiter le Louvre.

(In Paris you can visit the Louvre.)

Set up a French tourist information centre for children to role play questions and answers. If the children have learnt how to ask for and give directions, they can incorporate this into their role plays.

Où habites-tu?

J'habite à Londres,

C'est en Angleterre.

J'habite un appartement,

C'est au bord de la rivière.

Dis-moi, dis-moi!

Où est-ce que tu habites?

J'habite à Paris,

Paris est en France.

J'aime monter à la Tour Eiffel,

C'est très cool! J'ai de la chance!

Dis-moi, dis-moi!

Où est-ce que tu habites?

J'habite à Marseille,

Au bord de la mer.

J'aime pêcher avec mon oncle,

Les poissons, ils sont supers!

Dis-moi, dis-moi!

Où est-ce que tu habites?

J'habite à Bordeaux,

La région du vin.

Le vin blanc, rosé ou rouge,

Comme tu veux, les vins sont bons!

Dis-moi, dis-moi!

Où est-ce que tu habites?

Où habites-tu?

SINGING FRENCH © HELEN MACGREGOR & STEPHEN CHADWICK 2004, HarperCollins*Publishers* Ltd

photocopiable

Où est-il?

names of places in a town/understanding and giving directions

CD tracks   **27** the song   **28** backing track   **49** spoken phrases

Using the song

Begin by teaching the class the directions in the song and their meanings:

**Tournez à droite, tournez à gauche,
Allez tout droit et le/la voilà!**

Explain the use of the masculine and feminine in **le/la voilà** to match with the gender of the place name, eg

le marché, le stade (m) – **le voilà**

l'école, la piscine (f) – **la voilà**

Listen to the song (track 27) and all join in with the chanted directions. Then teach the verses either by listening to track 49 or by saying the words yourself for the children to copy. Make sure that the children know the meaning of the words. When everyone is confident, perform the whole song with the backing track (track 28).

Developing the vocabulary

Introduce the names of more places in a town, eg

la gare (the railway station)

la poste (the post office)

le port (the port)

la banque (the bank)

Invite the class to choose four different place names to use in the song. Sing the new version of the song with the backing track (track 28).

Extend the vocabulary of directions by composing a new chant, eg

**Allez tout droit, deuxième à gauche,
Troisième à droite et vous êtes là!**

(Go straight on, take the second road on the left,
The third road on the right and there you are!)

In pairs, the children prepare new versions of the song with their own choice of places and directions. Divide the class into two groups to perform some of the ideas, taking it in turns to ask for and give directions. Afterwards, some pairs may like to perform their own versions of the song to the class.

vocabulary

Où est-il? – Where is it?

où est – where is

le marché – the market

s'il vous plaît – please

répétez – repeat

tournez à droite – turn right

tournez à gauche – turn left

allez tout droit – go straight on

et – and

le voilà/la voilà – there it is

le stade – the stadium

l'école (une école) – the school (a school)

la piscine – the swimming pool

Follow-up work

Play **Suivez la route** (Follow the route). Set up an obstacle course in a large space, eg using bean bags in the school hall. Explain that the objective is to safely guide a blindfolded traveller along the route with verbal instructions, eg

Tout droit – slow steps forwards

Arrêtes!/Stop! – stand still

A gauche/à droite – turn to the left/right

Blindfold a volunteer and demonstrate giving instructions in French to safely guide them to the end of the route. Then invite confident individuals to give the instructions to guide other travellers along the route.

Divide the class into small groups, who each design a new route. Individuals take it in turns to guide a blindfolded traveller through.

Où est-il?

Où est … où est …
Où est le marché, s'il vous plaît?
(répétez)

Tournez à droite, tournez à gauche,
Allez tout droit et le voilà!

Où est … où est …
Où est le stade, s'il vous plaît? (répétez)

Tournez à droite, tournez à gauche,
Allez tout droit et le voilà!

Où est … où est …
Où est l'école, s'il vous plaît?
(répétez)

Tournez à droite, tournez à gauche,
Allez tout droit et la voilà!

Où est … où est …
Où est la piscine, s'il vous plaît?
(répétez)

Tournez à droite, tournez à gauche,
Allez tout droit et la voilà!

J'ai soif, j'ai faim

asking for drinks and snacks

Using the song

All listen to the song (track 29). Ask the children to identify any words they recognise, eg **un sandwich**. Teach a verse at a time either by listening to track 50 or by saying the words yourself for the children to copy. Ensure that the children know the meaning of each of the food items.

When everyone is familiar with the vocabulary, sing the whole song with the backing track (track 30).

Developing the vocabulary

Introduce vocabulary for other flavours of ice cream, eg

framboise (raspberry)

cassis (blackcurrant)

pistache (pistachio)

menthe (mint)

café (coffee)

noix de coco (coconut)

Invite four children to select flavours for a new version of verse one. All sing it with the backing track (track 30).

Extend the children's knowledge of food and drink vocabulary, eg

de l'eau minérale (some mineral water)

de la limonade (some lemonade)

du chocolat (some chocolate/hot chocolate)

du jus d'orange (some orange juice)

une crêpe au chocolat (a pancake with chocolate)

une crêpe à la confiture (a pancake with jam)

des chips (some crisps)

une banane (a banana)

une poire (a pear)

As a class, compose new versions of verses two to four, then sing the whole new song with the backing track.

vocabulary

j'ai soif – I'm thirsty

j'ai faim – I'm hungry

j'ai chaud – I'm hot

je voudrais – I would like

la glace (une glace) – ice cream (an ice cream)

vanille – vanilla

chocolat – chocolate

fraise – strawberry

citron – lemon

j'aime – I like

c'est bon – it's good/great

les boissons (une boisson) – drinks (a drink)

du thé – (some) tea

du café – (some) coffee

du coca – (some) cola

du lait – (some) milk

j'ai froid – I'm cold

les crêpes (une crêpe) – pancakes (a pancake)

nature – plain

au sucre – with sugar

à la banane – with banana

un goûter/le goûter – afternoon snack

un sandwich au fromage – a cheese sandwich

des frites – (some) chips

une pomme – an apple

Follow-up work

Provide French food packaging for the class to investigate more vocabulary for food and ingredients.

Play **Au café** (In the café). In small groups, the children compile and design café menus using the food and drink vocabulary they have learnt. Teach the following phrases:

Que désirez-vous? (What would you like?) **Avec quoi?** (Anything else?)

In small groups, the children take it in turns to play the role of waiter/waitress (**le garçon/la serveuse**) and customers. Each waiter/waitress invites individuals to order food and drink from the menus, writing down the orders if desired.

Point out that the 'customers' will need to use **un** instead of **du** when ordering drinks, eg

Je voudrais un jus d'orange.

J'ai soif, j'ai faim

J'ai chaud, j'ai soif,

Je voudrais une glace.

Vanille, chocolat, fraise, citron,

J'aime la glace. Mmmm, c'est bon!

J'ai chaud, j'ai soif,

Je voudrais une boisson.

Du thé, du café, du coca, du lait,

J'aime les boissons. Mmmm, c'est bon!

J'ai froid, j'ai faim,

Je voudrais une crêpe.

Nature, au sucre, à la banane,

J'aime les crêpes. Mmmm, c'est bon!

J'ai froid, j'ai faim,

Je voudrais un goûter.

Un sandwich au fromage, des frites, une pomme,

J'aime le goûter. Mmmm, c'est bon!

A la boulangerie

French money/names of places in a town

Using the song

All listen to the song (track 31). Ask the children if they can recognise any of the items being bought, or their prices. Teach the verses either by listening to track 51 or by saying the words yourself for the children to copy. Ensure that the children understand the name of each shop.

When everyone is familiar with the vocabulary, sing the song in unison with the backing track (track 32).

If you wish, divide the class into two groups to sing the parts of shopkeeper and customer. All sing the first line of each verse. Swap parts so that everyone has a chance to practise each role.

Developing the vocabulary

Introduce vocabulary for other food items that might be bought in the shops mentioned, eg

un pain (a loaf)

un croissant

un pain au chocolat

une tarte aux pommes (apple tart)

des saucisses (some sausages)

du pâté (some paté)

de la viande (some meat)

des œufs (some eggs)

du poisson (some fish)

des moules (some mussels)

Make price labels for some of the items. Invite confident individuals to say the prices in French and translate them.

In pairs, children practise a role play using the structure of the shopping role play in the song, but substituting their own choice of foods and prices. The role plays could then be performed to the class.

vocabulary

à – at/in

la boulangerie – the baker's

je voudrais – I would like

une baguette – a baguette

s'il vous plaît – please

Voilà! – Here you are!

C'est combien? – How much is it?/ How much is that?

un euro – one euro

Merci Madame/Monsieur! – Thank you! (used when addressing an adult)

Au revoir! – Goodbye!

la pâtisserie – the cake shop

deux gâteaux (un gâteau) – two cakes (a cake)

neuf euros dix – nine euros ten

la charcuterie – the delicatessen

du jambon – some ham

trois euros vingt – three euros twenty

la poissonnerie – the fish shop

des crevettes – some prawns

désolé/e – I'm sorry (m/f)

je n'en ai plus – I haven't any left

bien – well then/fine

à demain – see you tomorrow

Follow-up work

Discuss typical French food customs, such as buying fresh bread every day, drinking hot chocolate from a bowl at breakfast time, buying cakes from the baker's on Sundays and eating **une bûche de Noël** (a Yule log) at Christmas.

The class could research the types of French foods available in British supermarkets, eg cheese, butter, biscuits, fruit, vegetables, bottled water, wine.

Have a French food tasting day. Encourage the children to prepare foods and label them. They can then take it in turns to offer food to their classmates, eg **Tu voudrais du camembert?**

A la boulangerie

A la boulangerie, la boulangerie,
'Je voudrais une baguette, s'il vous plaît.'
'Voilà!'   'C'est combien?'
'Un euro.'   'Merci Madame,
Au revoir!'

A la pâtisserie, la pâtisserie,
'Je voudrais deux gâteaux, s'il vous plaît.'
'Voilà!'   'C'est combien?'
'Neuf euros dix.'   'Merci Monsieur,
Au revoir!'

A la charcuterie, la charcuterie,
'Je voudrais du jambon, s'il vous plaît.'
'Voilà!'   'C'est combien?'
'Trois euros vingt.'   'Merci Madame,
Au revoir!'

A la poissonnerie, la poissonnerie,
'Je voudrais des crevettes, s'il vous plaît.'
'Désolé, je n'en ai plus.'
'Bien, à demain. Merci Monsieur,
Au revoir!'

photocopiable

La météo

weather phrases/points of the compass

Using the song

Enlarge and display this map of France. Listen to the song (track 33), pointing to the north, south, west and east on the map during the line **Au nord, au sud, à l'ouest et à l'est**. All join in singing this line each time it occurs.

Learn the phrases for the first two lines of each verse, either using track 52 or by saying the words yourself for the children to copy. All join in each time these phrases are repeated.

When everyone is confident, sing the whole song first with track 33 and then with the backing track (track 34).

Developing the vocabulary

Introduce more weather vocabulary, eg

il fait du soleil (it is sunny)

il fait mauvais (the weather is bad)

un orage (a thunderstorm)

Photocopy and cut out the weather symbols on the song sheet. As a class, choose four symbols to fix to the map of France in the north, south, west and east. All chant the weather forecast you have created, eg

Au nord il fait chaud,
Au sud il pleut,
A l'ouest il y a un orage,
A l'est il y a du vent.
Au nord, au sud, à l'ouest et à l'est,
La météo aujourd'hui, mon ami!

vocabulary

la météo – the weather forecast
il fait beau – the weather is fine
aujourd'hui – today
il fait chaud – it is warm
au nord – in the north
au sud – in the south
à l'ouest – in the west
et – and
à l'est – in the east
mon ami/e – my friend (m/f)
il fait froid – it is cold
il neige – it is snowing
il y a du vent – it is windy
il pleut – it is raining

Follow-up work

Invite individuals to prepare and present their own weather forecast to the class using the map of France and the weather symbols. You might like to introduce the phrase **au centre** (in the centre) as an alternative way of starting a sentence. The children could also be encouraged to use the place names that appear on the map, eg

A Paris il fait du soleil.

A Toulouse il neige.

Practise weather vocabulary daily by asking the class questions, eg

Aujourd'hui c'est lundi. Quel temps fait-il?

(Today is Monday. What is the weather like?)

If possible, video a French weather forecast and show it to the class. Ask the children if they recognise any words or phrases.

La météo

Il fait beau aujourd'hui,

Il fait chaud aujourd'hui.

Il fait beau aujourd'hui,

Il fait chaud aujourd'hui.

Au nord, au sud, à l'ouest et à l'est,

Il fait beau aujourd'hui, mon ami!

Il fait froid aujourd'hui,

Il neige aujourd'hui.

Il fait froid aujourd'hui,

Il neige aujourd'hui.

Au nord, au sud, à l'ouest et à l'est,

Il fait froid aujourd'hui, mon ami!

Il y a du vent aujourd'hui,

Il pleut aujourd'hui.

Il y a du vent aujourd'hui,

Il pleut aujourd'hui.

Au nord, au sud, à l'ouest et à l'est,

Il y a du vent aujourd'hui, mon ami!

Les vacances
names of countries/asking and saying where someone is going

Using the song

Listen to the song (track 35), then teach the class the chorus (**Pendant les vacances ...**) using track 53 or by saying the words yourself for the children to copy.

Listen to the song again and ask the children if they can identify any of the countries sung by the male singer. Teach the names of the countries, then practise the responses by calling out the countries one by one for the class to reply with the appropriate rhyming phrases.

When everyone is familiar with the vocabulary, perform the song together, first with track 35 and then with the backing track (track 36). Sing the chorus together and divide into two groups to perform the countries and reponses. Swap over so that everyone has a chance to sing each part.

Developing the vocabulary

Play **Autour du monde** (Around the world). Make a set of eight cards showing the names of each country from the song (**En Afrique**, **En Belgique** and so on). Shuffle the cards and place them face down.

Invite eight individuals to select a card, keeping it hidden from the class. They stand in a line and in turn call out the name of the country on the card. The class responds with the matching rhyming phrase.

Practise all eight countries and responses in the new sequence. Then perform the song with the backing track (track 36), substituting the new sequence of countries.

When everyone is familiar with the activity, repeat with another eight individuals. This time, perform the song immediately with the backing track.

Introduce the class to names of other countries, eg
au pays de Galles (in Wales)
en Ecosse (in Scotland)
en Irlande du Nord (in Northern Ireland)
en Allemagne (in Germany)
aux Etats-Unis (in the United States)

vocabulary

les vacances – the holidays
pendant – during/in
je vais – I go/I am going
en France – to France
Oh là là! – exclamation, eg Oh my goodness!
en bateau – by boat
et – and
en auto – by car
je vais manger – I'm going to eat
des escargots – snails
Où vas-tu? – Where are you going?
en Afrique – to Africa
c'est magnifique – it's magnificent
en Belgique – to Belgium
c'est fantastique – it's fantasic
en Espagne – to Spain
à la montagne – in the mountains
au Japon – to Japan
c'est bon – it's great
en Italie – to Italy
pour faire du ski – to ski
en Australie – to Australia
c'est loin d'ici – it's a long way away
aux Pays-Bas – to the Netherlands
ça va, ça va – good, good
en Russie – to Russia
mais – but
ça suffit – that's enough

Follow-up work

Discuss the origins of names of countries, eg **Angleterre** – land of the Angles. Explain that **la terre** means 'land' or 'earth' and **un pays** is 'a country'.

Ask the children to research the flags of the countries they know in French, using books and/or the internet. They could draw or collect pictures for a class display.

Hold a Eurovision song contest, with groups of children representing different countries as they perform **Les vacances**. After each performance the other groups award marks out of ten, eg **L'Allemagne – huit points** (Germany – eight points). Record the points and find the totals to establish the winning group!

Les vacances

Pendant les vacances, je vais en France, oh là là!

Je vais en France pendant les vacances, oh là là!

En bateau et en auto.

Je vais manger des escargots!

Pendant les vacances, je vais en France, oh là là!

Pendant les vacances, où vas-tu?

Où vas-tu, pendant les vacances?

En Afrique	C'est magnifique!
En Belgique	C'est fantastique!
En Espagne	A la montagne
Au Japon	Ah oui, c'est bon!

En Italie	Pour faire du ski
En Australie	C'est loin d'ici!
Aux Pays-Bas	Ça va, ça va!
En Russie	Mais ça suffit!

Pendant les vacances, je vais en France, oh là là ...

SINGING FRENCH © HELEN MACGREGOR & STEPHEN CHADWICK 2004, HarperCollins*Publishers* Ltd

Aller à l'école

saying where someone is going

CD tracks   **37** the song   **38** backing track   **54** spoken phrases

Using the song

All listen to the song (track 37), joining in with the last two lines of each verse as they become familiar.

Teach the verses one at a time, either by listening to track 54 or by saying the words yourself for the children to copy. Draw attention to the way the verb **aller** changes throughout the song and explain the use of **on va** (impersonal) to mean 'everyone goes' or 'we go'. Discuss how **ils vont** is used for an all-male group or when the group includes both males and females. **Elles vont** is used only for an all-female group.

When everyone is familiar with the vocabulary, sing the whole song with the backing track (track 38).

Developing the vocabulary

To extend the vocabulary of place names, ask the children to suggest new places to visit in each verse, eg

à la piscine (to the swimming pool)

à l'hôtel (to the hotel)

à l'église (to church)

au tabac (to the tobacconist)

en ville (to town)

à Paris (to Paris)

à Londres (to London)

Substitute new places according to the children's suggestions and all sing the new version with the backing track (track 38).

Introduce vocabulary for other means of transport, eg

en autobus (by bus)

en autocar (by coach)

par le train (by train)

en avion/par avion (by aeroplane)

en bateau (by boat)

Sing another new version of the song with the backing track, substituting new means of transport as well as new places.

vocabulary

aller – to go/going

à l'école – to school

je vais – I go

à pied – on foot

tu vas – you go

à vélo – by bicycle

quand – when

il fait beau – the weather is fine

il pleut – it rains/it is raining

on va – everyone goes/we go

en auto – by car

il/elle va – he/she goes

à la poste – to the post office

nous allons – we go

au café – to the café

vous allez – you go (polite/plural)

ils/elles vont – they go (m/f)

à la gare – to the railway station

Follow-up work

Carry out a class survey of the means of transport used to travel to school. Ask individuals around the class **Comment est-ce que tu viens à l'école?** (How do you come to school?).

The individuals reply giving the means of transport they use, eg

Je viens à l'école en autobus et à pied.

Make a tally chart to record the number of children who use each means of transport. Draw a class bar chart on paper or on a computer and encourage the children to discuss the totals in French.

Aller à l'école

Je vais à l'école à pied,

Tu vas à l'école à vélo.

A pied, à vélo, quand il fait beau;

Quand il pleut, on va en auto!

Il va à la poste à pied,

Elle va à la poste à vélo.

A pied, à vélo, quand il fait beau;

Quand il pleut, on va en auto!

Nous allons au café à pied,

Vous allez au café à vélo.

A pied, à vélo, quand il fait beau;

Quand il pleut, on va en auto!

Ils vont à la gare à pied,

Elles vont à la gare à vélo.

A pied, à vélo, quand il fait beau;

Quand il pleut, on va en auto!

SINGING FRENCH © HELEN MACGREGOR & STEPHEN CHADWICK 2004, HarperCollins*Publishers* Ltd

Le football

names of sports/stating likes and dislikes

Using the song

All listen to the song (track 39) and join in with the chanted spelling of **f-o-o-t-b-a-l-l** each time it is repeated. Ask the children to identify any other sports or leisure activities they recognise in the song.

Teach the first verse, either by listening to track 55 or by saying the words yourself for the children to copy. Then teach the phrases for the second and third verses. All sing the whole song, first with track 39 and then with the backing track (track 40).

Developing the vocabulary

Explain to the class that it is more common to use the abbreviation **le foot** than **le football** when in conversation with friends, eg **J'adore jouer au foot!**

Make a list on the board of the children's favourite sports and hobbies, extending the vocabulary as required, eg

jouer aux échecs (to play chess)

écouter de la musique (to listen to music)

faire du ski (to ski)

faire de la gymnastique (to do gymnastics)

nager (to swim)

pêcher (to fish)

lire (to read)

In pairs, the children discuss the sports and activities they like best and those they do not like. Introduce the phrases **J'aime bien ...** (I really like ...) and **Je déteste ...** (I hate ...).

Carry out a class survey of how many children like each of the sports and activities. As a class, make a bar chart of the most and least popular activities.

Follow-up work

Make a class sports and hobbies magazine. Begin by asking the children to look at magazines and/or the internet to find names and pictures of French sports personalities and teams.

Working in groups, the children produce adverts, pictures and captions, using ICT if possible. They can make up details of sports events, giving times, dates and venues to incorporate vocabulary previously learnt.

Encourage the children to use dictionaries to look up other sport-related vocabulary they may need, eg

une équipe (a team)

un joueur/une joueuse de tennis (a tennis player, m/f)

la Coupe du monde (the World Cup)

As a class, choose a title for the magazine.

Le football

F-O-O-T-B-A-L-L F-O-O-T-B-A-L-L F-O-O-T-B-A-L-L

J'adore jouer au football!

J'aime jouer au basket,

J'aime jouer aux cartes.

J'aime regarder la télé,

J'aime faire du cheval.

Mais j'adore jouer au football!

F-O-O-T-B-A-L-L F-O-O-T-B-A-L-L F-O-O-T-B-A-L-L ...

Ma copine, Sylvie,

Elle aime jouer au tennis.

Mon copain, Rachid,

Il aime jouer au rugby.

Mais ils adorent jouer au football!

F-O-O-T-B-A-L-L F-O-O-T-B-A-L-L F-O-O-T-B-A-L-L ...

Ma copine, Zineb,

Elle n'aime pas jouer au tennis.

Mon copain, Christophe,

Il n'aime pas jouer au rugby.

Mais ils adorent jouer au football!

F-O-O-T-B-A-L-L F-O-O-T-B-A-L-L F-O-O-T-B-A-L-L ...

photocopiable

Quelle heure est-il?

asking and saying the time/names of school subjects

Using the song

Listen to the song (track 41) and all join in with the chorus. At the beginning of each verse, show the class a clock face set to the correct time. Ask the children if they can guess or recognise any of the activities described in the verses.

Teach the verses one at a time, either by listening to track 56 or by saying the words yourself for the children to copy. You could use an enlarged photocopy of the song sheet to help the class remember some of the activities.

When everyone is confident, sing the whole song with the backing track (track 42).

Developing the vocabulary

Use a clock face to gradually introduce more time vocabulary, eg

une heure et demie (half past one)

six heures et quart (quarter past six)

deux heures moins le quart (quarter to two)

Also tell the class the names of other school subjects, eg

les maths/les mathématiques (maths)

l'histoire (history)

la géographie (geography)

la musique (music)

le sport (sport/games)

la technologie (technology/DT)

le dessin (art)

As a class, compose new verses for the song, choosing different times of day and using activity phrases the children have already learnt, eg

Il est huit heures
Huit heures du matin.
Je bois du chocolat (I drink some hot chocolate)
Et je mange du pain. (And I eat some bread.)

Sing the new version of the song with the backing track (track 42).

vocabulary

Quelle heure est-il? – What time is it?

le matin – morning

le soir – evening

le jour – day

la nuit – night

midi – midday

ou – or

minuit – midnight

il est sept heures – it is seven o'clock

sept heures du matin – seven o'clock in the morning

je me lève – I get up

je me lave – I have a wash

dans – in

la salle de bains – the bathroom

l'école commence – school is starting

j'ai – I have

(l')anglais – English

(le) français – French

et – and

après – afterwards

(les) sciences – science

c'est – it is

j'aime bien – I like

déjeuner – to have lunch

avec mes amis – with my friends

maintenant – now

je dîne – I have dinner/supper

je me couche – I go to bed

à dix heures moins le quart – at quarter to ten

Follow-up work

Ask the children to draw a cartoon strip of the activities they do throughout the day, with pictures of clocks showing the time. Invite individuals to present their work to the class, saying the times and describing the activities they have recorded, eg

Il est huit heures moins le quart. Je prends le petit déjeuner.

(It is quarter to eight. I have breakfast.)

Il est deux heures. J'ai histoire.

(It is two o'clock. I have history.)

Il est cinq heures et demie. J'écoute de la musique.

(It is half past five. I listen to music.)

Quelle heure est-il?

Quelle heure est-il? Quelle heure est-il?

Le matin, le soir, le jour, la nuit.

Quelle heure est-il? Quelle heure est-il?

Midi ou minuit? Midi ou minuit?

Il est sept heures,

Sept heures du matin.

Je me lève, je me lave,

Dans la salle de bains.

Il est neuf heures,

L'école commence.

J'ai anglais, j'ai français

Et après j'ai sciences.

Quelle heure est-il? Quelle heure est-il ...

Il est douze heures,

Douze heures, c'est midi.

Et j'aime bien déjeuner

Avec mes amis.

Il est six heures,

Maintenant, c'est le soir.

Et je dîne, je me couche

A dix heures moins le quart.

Quelle heure est-il? Quelle heure est-il ...

SINGING FRENCH © HELEN MACGREGOR & STEPHEN CHADWICK 2004, HarperCollins*Publishers* Ltd

La machine à laver

names of items of clothing/colours

CD tracks    **43** the song   **44** backing track   **57** spoken phrases

Using the song

All listen to the song (track 43) and join in with the rock 'n' roll line as it becomes familiar (**Rock 'n' roll, pêle-mêle, rond, rond, rond …**). Listen to the song again and teach the chorus using track 57 or by saying the words yourself for the children to copy. Finally, teach the lines which describe the items of clothing.

When the class is familiar with the whole song, sing it with the backing track (track 44). The children may wish to devise a dance or actions to perform as they sing.

Developing the vocabulary

Introduce the class to more vocabulary for items of clothing, eg

un chapeau (a hat)

une chemise (a shirt)

un jean (a pair of jeans)

un pull (a jumper)

des chaussures (shoes)

Also introduce other adjectives to describe clothing, eg

grand/e (large, m/f)   **petit/e** (small, m/f)

long/ue (long, m/f)   **court/e** (short, m/f)

joli/e (pretty, m/f)

Discuss that an 'e' (or 'ue' for **long**) is added to these adjectives when the noun is feminine. This may affect the way the word is pronounced, eg **un pull grand** (m), **une chemise grande** (f). An 's' is added for plural nouns, eg **les pulls grands** (m plural), **les chemises grandes** (f plural). Most colours follow the same rules. However, irregular ones include **blanc/blanche** (white, m/f), **violet/violette** (purple, m/f) and **marron** (brown), which never changes.

Ask small groups or pairs to think of four new items to create a new verse for the song, eg

Un pull grand, un chapeau bleu,
Un jean long, une chemise jolie.

All perform some of the new verses with the backing track (track 44).

vocabulary

la machine à laver – the washing machine

dans – in

avec – with

de l'eau chaude – (some) warm water

et – and

de la lessive – (some) washing powder

tous – all (m, plural)

les vêtements – the clothes

(ils) dansent – (they) dance

ils se disent – they say to themselves

c'est amusant – this is fun

rock 'n' roll – rock and roll

pêle-mêle – jumbled up

rond – round

un sweatshirt – a sweatshirt

bleu – blue

des chaussettes (une chaussette) – socks (a sock)

noir – black

un T-shirt – a T-shirt

blanc/blanche – white (m/f)

un pantalon – a pair of trousers

une jupe – a skirt

rose – pink

une robe – a dress

jaune – yellow

un short – a pair of shorts

vert – green

un pullover – a pullover

Follow-up work

Teach the class the phrases **je porte** (I am wearing) and **il/elle porte** (he/she is wearing).

Hold a class fashion show. Select children to model items of clothing and a presenter to describe what is being worn, eg

Sunita porte une jupe jolie, une chemise noire et des chaussures blanches.

Allow children to take turns to do the presenting.

Ask the children to cut out pictures of famous people from magazines and to describe what they are wearing. Their appearance can also be described once the appropriate vocabulary has been learnt, eg

Il s'appelle Thierry Henry. Il a les cheveux courts et les yeux marron.
Il porte un T-shirt rouge.

(His name is Thierry Henry. He has short hair and brown eyes. He is wearing a red T-shirt.)

La machine à laver

Dans la machine à laver,

Avec de l'eau chaude et de la lessive,

Tous les vêtements dansent.

Ils se disent, 'C'est amusant!'

Rock 'n' roll, pêle-mêle, rond, rond, rond,

Dans la machine à laver.

Un sweatshirt bleu, des chaussettes noires,

Un T-shirt blanc et un pantalon.

Rock 'n' roll, pêle-mêle, rond, rond, rond.

Rock 'n' roll, pêle-mêle, rond, rond, rond.

Rock 'n' roll, pêle-mêle, rond, rond, rond.

Rock 'n' roll, pêle-mêle, rond, rond, rond, rond.

Dans la machine à laver ...

Une jupe rose, une robe jaune,

Un short vert et un pullover.

Rock 'n' roll, pêle-mêle, rond, rond, rond.

Rock 'n' roll, pêle-mêle, rond, rond, rond.

Rock 'n' roll, pêle-mêle, rond, rond, rond.

Rock 'n' roll, pêle-mêle, rond, rond, rond, rond.

Dans la machine à laver ...

Dans la machine à laver!

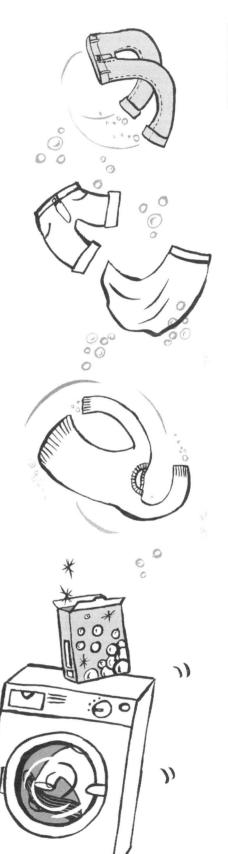

SINGING FRENCH © HELEN MACGREGOR & STEPHEN CHADWICK 2004, HarperCollins*Publishers* Ltd

Melody lines

1 **Bonjour** (p6)

3 **Comment t'appelles-tu?** (p8)

5 **Un deux trois** (p10)

7 A douze (p12)

Un deux trois quatre cinq six sept huit neuf dix. Un deux trois
quatre cinq six sept huit neuf dix. Un deux trois quatre cinq six
sept huit neuf dix onze douze. Un deux trois quatre cinq six sept huit neuf
dix Un deux trois quatre cinq six sept huit neuf dix.

9 Ma trousse (p14)

Dans ma trousse, j'ai un sty - lo. Dans ma trousse, j'ai un sty - lo.

1. Un sty - lo pour é - crire.

2. Un cray - on Et un sty - lo pour é - crire.

3. Un taille - cray - on, un cray - on Et un sty - lo pour é - crire.

4. U - ne gomme, un taille - cray - on, un cray - on Et un sty - lo pour é - crire.

5. U - ne règle, u - ne gomme, un taille - cray - on, un cray - on Et un sty - lo pour é - crire.

Melody lines

11 La semaine (p16)

Lun - di mar - di mer - cre - di jeu - di ven - dre - di same - di di - manche

Un deux trois quatre cinq six sept, Les sept jours de la se - maine. Un deux trois quatre cinq six sept,

Les sept jours de la se - maine. Lun - di mar - di

mer - cre - di jeu - di ven - dre - di same - di di - manche (dimanche)

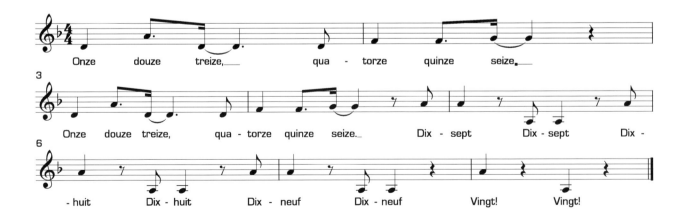

13 Onze à vingt (p18)

Onze douze treize, ___ qua - torze quinze seize. ___

Onze douze treize, qua - torze quinze seize. ___ Dix - sept Dix - sept Dix -

- huit Dix - huit Dix - neuf Dix - neuf Vingt! Vingt!

15 L'alphabet (p20)

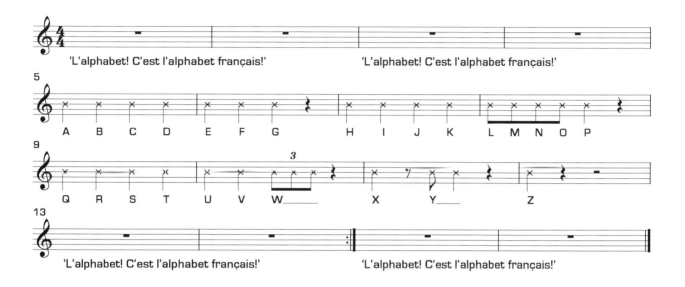

'L'alphabet! C'est l'alphabet français!'   'L'alphabet! C'est l'alphabet français!'

A B C D E F G   H I J K L M N O P

Q R S T U V W   X Y Z

'L'alphabet! C'est l'alphabet français!'   'L'alphabet! C'est l'alphabet français!'

17 Ma famille (p22)

Père, mère, sœur, frère.   C'est ma fa - mille,_

c'est moi!   C'est la fa - mille_ Pe - tit,   c'est ma fa - mille!_

Je te pré - sente mon père.   Bon - jour Mon - sieur Pe - tit!   Je te pré - sente ma mère.

Bon - jour Ma - dame Pe - tit!   Je te pré - sente ma sœur, Sté - pha - nie.   Sa - lut Sté - pha - nie!

Je te pré - sente mon frère, Lu - ci - en.   Sa - lut Lu - ci - en!   C'est ma fa - mille,_

c'est moi!   C'est la fa - mille_ Pe - tit,   c'est ma fa - mille!_

Melody lines

19 Mon monstre (p24)

J'ai un co-pain, un bon co-pain u-nique, vrai, u-nique!

Quand je suis seul, je le fais moi-même, C'est

la mé-thode sci-en-ti-fique, mé-thode sci-en-ti-fique. Quand je suis seul, je le

to Coda

fais moi-même, C'est la mé-thode sci-en-ti-fique, mé-thode sci-en-ti-fique.

Mon monstre a une tête, Qua-tre bras et six or-eilles.
Mon monstre a qua-tre mains, Deux jambes et deux pieds.

D.C. al Coda

Mon monstre a une bouche, Cinq dents, huit yeux et trois nez.

CODA

J'ai un co-pain, un bon co-pain u-nique, vrai. u-nique!

21 Zéro à cent (p26)

Melody lines

23 Joyeux anniversaire (p28)

Quelle est la date de ton an-ni-ver-saire? Quelle est la date de ton an-ni-ver-saire? Au prin-

temps, en é-té, en au-tomne, en hiv-er? Quelle est la date de ton an-ni-ver-saire?

FINE

Jan-vi-er (Oui!) Joy-eux an-ni-ver-saire! Fév-ri-er (Oui!) Joy-eux an-ni-ver-saire! etc.

D.C. al Fine

25 Où habites-tu? (p30)

J'ha-bite à Lon-dres, C'est en An-gle-terre.

J'ha-bite un ap-par-te-ment, C'est au bord de la ri-vière. Dis-moi, dis-moi!

Où est-ce que tu ha-bites? Où ha-bites-tu?

27 Où est-il? (p32)

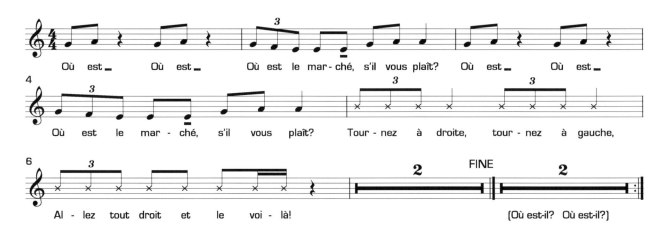

Où est _ Où est _ Où est le mar-ché, s'il vous plaît? Où est _ Où est _

Où est le mar-ché, s'il vous plaît? Tour-nez à droite, tour-nez à gauche,

Al-lez tout droit et le voi-là! FINE (Où est-il? Où est-il?)

56

29 J'ai soif, j'ai faim (p34)

J'ai chaud, j'ai soif, Je vou-drais une glace. Va - nille, cho - co - lat,

fraise, ci - tron, J'aime la glace. Mmmm, c'est bon!

31 A la boulangerie (p36)

A la bou - lan - ge - rie,___ la bou - lan - ge - rie,___ 'Je vou-drais une ba-guette, s'il vous

plaît.' 'Voi - là!' 'C'est com-bien?' 'Un___ eu - ro.' 'Mer - ci Ma-

-dame, Au re - voir!' A la pois-son-ne-rie,___ la pois-son-ne-rie.___ 'Je

vou-drais des cre-vettes, s'il vous plaît.' 'Dé - so - lé, je n'en ai plus.'

'Bien, à de-main. Mer - ci Mon -sieur, Au re - voir!'

Melody lines

33 La météo (p38)

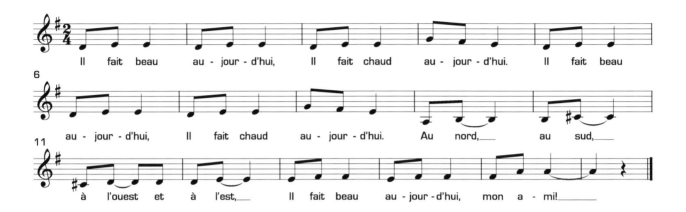

35 Les vacances (p40)

37 Aller à l'école (p42)

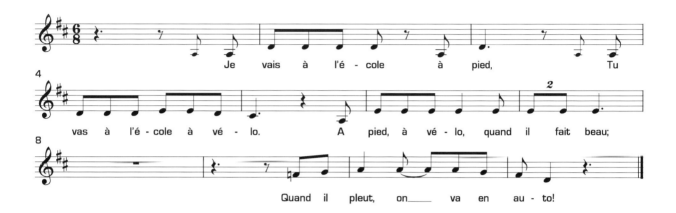

Je vais à l'é - cole à pied, Tu
vas à l'é - cole à vé - lo. A pied, à vé - lo, quand il fait beau;
Quand il pleut, on___ va en au - to!

39 Le football (p44)

F O O T B A L L F O O T B A L L F O O T
B A L L J'a - dore jou - er au foot - ball! J'aime jou - er au bas - ket,
J'aime jou - er aux cartes. J'aime re - gar - der la té - lé,
J'aime faire du che - val.___ Mais j'a - dore jou - er au foot - ball!
F O O T B A L L F O O T B A L L
F O O T B A L L J'a - dore jou - er au foot - ball!

Melody lines

41 Quelle heure est-il? (p46)

Quelle heure est - il?   Quelle heure est - il?

Le ma - tin,   le soir,   le jour, la nuit.

Quelle heure est - il?   Quelle heure est - il?

FINE

Mi - di ou min - uit?   Mi - di ou min - uit?

Il est sept heures,   Sept heures du ma - tin.
Il est douze heures,   Douze heures, c'est mi - di.

Je me lève,   je me lave,   Dans la salle de
Et j'aime bien   dé - jeu - ner   A - vec mes a -

bains.   Il est neuf heures, L'é - cole com - mence.
- mis.   Il est six heures, Main - te - nant, c'est le soir.

D.C. al Fine

J'ai ang - lais,   j'ai fran - çais   Et a - près j'ai sci - ences.
Et je dîne,   je me couche   A dix heures moins le quart.

43 La machine à laver (p48)

Dans la ma-chine à la - ver, A-vec de l'eau chaude et de la les-sive,_

Tous les vête-ments dansent. Ils se disent, 'C'est a - mu - sant!'_

to Coda

Rock 'n' roll, pêle-mêle, rond, rond, rond,_ Dans la ma-chine à la - ver. Un

sweat-shirt bleu, des chaus-settes noires, Un T - shirt blanc Et un pan - ta - lon.

Rock 'n' roll, pêle-mêle, rond, rond, rond._ Rock 'n' roll, pêle-mêle, rond, rond, rond.

Rock 'n' roll, pêle-mêle, rond, rond, rond._ Rock 'n' roll, pêle-mêle, rond, rond, rond, rond.

2.

Dans la ma-chine à la - ver. Une jupe rose, une robe jaune,

Un short vert et un pull-o-ver. Rock 'n' roll, pêle-mêle, rond, rond, rond.

Rock 'n' roll, pêle-mêle, rond, rond, rond._ Rock 'n' roll, pêle-mêle, rond, rond, rond.

D.C. al Coda **CODA**

Rock 'n' roll, pêle-mêle, rond, rond, rond, rond. Dans la ma-chine à la -

ver, Dans la ma-chine à la - ver! (Ooh.)

Number cards

0   1

2   3

4   5

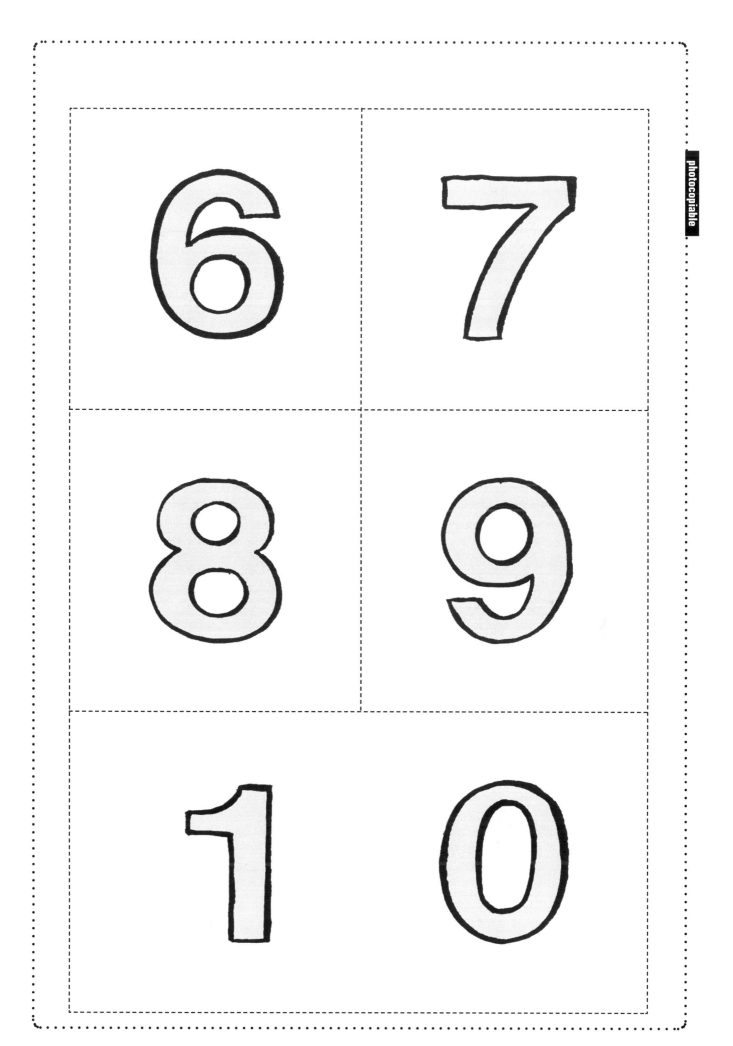

CD track list

Track Contents

1	**Bonjour** (p6)
2	**Bonjour** backing track
3	**Comment t'appelles-tu?** (p8)
4	**Comment t'appelles-tu?** backing track
5	**Un deux trois** (p10)
6	**Un deux trois** backing track
7	**A douze** (p12)
8	**A douze** backing track
9	**Ma trousse** (p14)
10	**Ma trousse** backing track
11	**La semaine** (p16)
12	**La semaine** backing track
13	**Onze à vingt** (p18)
14	**Onze à vingt** backing track
15	**L'alphabet** (p20)
16	**L'alphabet** backing track
17	**Ma famille** (p22)
18	**Ma famille** backing track
19	**Mon monstre** (p24)
20	**Mon monstre** backing track
21	**Zéro à cent** (p26)
22	**Zéro à cent** backing track
23	**Joyeux anniversaire** (p28)
24	**Joyeux anniversaire** backing track
25	**Où habites-tu?** (p30)
26	**Où habites-tu?** backing track
27	**Où est-il?** (p32)
28	**Où est-il?** backing track
29	**J'ai soif, j'ai faim** (p34)
30	**J'ai soif, j'ai faim** backing track
31	**A la boulangerie** (p36)
32	**A la boulangerie** backing track

Track Contents

33	**La météo** (p38)
34	**La météo** backing track
35	**Les vacances** (p40)
36	**Les vacances** backing track
37	**Aller à l'école** (p42)
38	**Aller à l'école** backing track
39	**Le football** (p44)
40	**Le football** backing track
41	**Quelle heure est-il?** (p46)
42	**Quelle heure est-il?** backing track
43	**La machine à laver** (p48)
44	**La machine à laver** backing track

Teaching tracks

Spoken vocabulary to help teach key words and phrases

Track Contents

45	**Ma trousse** (p14)
46	**Mon monstre** (p24)
47	**Joyeux anniversaire** (p28)
48	**Où habites-tu?** (p30)
49	**Où est-il?** (p32)
50	**J'ai soif, j'ai faim** (p34)
51	**A la boulangerie** (p36)
52	**La météo** (p38)
53	**Les vacances** (p40)
54	**Aller à l'école** (p42)
55	**Le football** (p44)
56	**Quelle heure est-il?** (p46)
57	**La machine à laver** (p48)

Acknowledgements

The authors and publishers would like to thank the following people for their help in the preparation of this resource: Hazel Bartlett, Camila Bataille, Mehdi Benjelloun, Diane Boisgibault, Françoise Evans, Nicolas Favey, Jeanne Fisher, Constance Gault, Jean-Pierre Giraud, Juliette Hawke, Megan Jenkins, Jocelyn Lucas, Adrien Malfevays, Marie Martin, Kerry Phipps, Lucy Poddington, Cath Rasbash, Ann Smith, Samuel Van Damme and Emily Wilson.

Special thanks are due to the staff and pupils of the Lycée Français Charles de Gaulle in London.